ZAHI HAWAS

HIGHLIGHTS
OF THE
EGYPTIAN MUSEUM

PHOTOGRAPHS BY SANDRO VANNINI

The American University in Cairo Press
Cairo - New York

First published in Egypt in 2010 by
The American University in Cairo Press
113 Sharia Kasr el Aini, Cairo, Egypt
420 Fifth Avenue, New York, NY 10018
www.aucpress.com

Dar el Kutub No. 11967/10
ISBN 978 977 416 438 5

Dar el Kutub Cataloging-in-Publication Data

Hawass, Zahi
        Highlights of the Egyptian Museum / Zahi Hawass.—Cairo: The American University in Cairo Press,
2010
        p.   cm.
        ISBN 978 977 416 438 5
        1. Egypt—Antiquities   I. Title
        932

1 2 3 4 5 6   15 14 13 12 11 10

Produced by Laboratoriorosso srl – Viterbo, Italy
Production and project manager Luca Vannini
Edited by Eve Byrne, Garry Shaw
Photography postproduction by Massimo Luciani
Graphic design by Silvia Cruciani – Studio Frasi
Printed and bound EBS Editoriale Bortolazzi – Stei, Verona, Italy

The Egyptian Museum in Cairo is a magical place. The moment you enter, you will be surrounded by five thousand years of history, and will feel the mystery and magnificence of ancient Egypt. Each statue, coffin, or stela that graces its galleries tells us not only about the distant past but also of the more recent time when it was uncovered from beneath the sands of Egypt. Although their stories are unwritten, each object is made even more priceless by the thrill of its discovery.

Many people complain to me that the Egyptian Museum is like a storehouse crammed with thousands of artifacts. I tell them that this was explained over a hundred years ago, when the museum was built, by the great French director of the Antiquities Service, Gaston Maspero. He said that the crowded appearance of the museum was a reflection of what was then modern Egyptian culture—in a modern Egyptian house of those times, you would find every inch of wall space crammed with photos and family mementos. This is exactly how the Cairo Museum is designed, but with pharaonic artifacts. However, today Egyptian houses are very different. This is one reason we are building the Grand Egyptian Museum by the pyramids at Giza; another is to make room for the thousands of artifacts that have been discovered since the Egyptian Museum was built. It is the dream of any archaeologist to see the artifacts that he or she has discovered on display at the Egyptian Museum. I know, because I am one of them. My dream has come true, and the most spectacular of the objects I have found in my excavations at Giza and Saqqara are in the museum now.

One of my earliest discoveries at Giza was a basalt statue of the dwarf Perniankhu. I will never forget two things about this discovery. The first was the appearance of the statue itself: the face and the modeling of the musculature made the statue come alive for me.

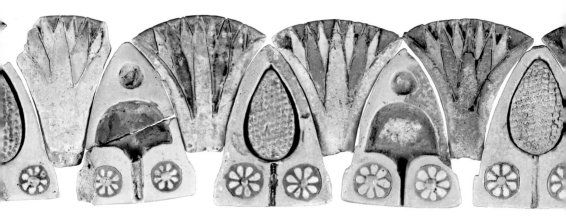

The second is the moment when I compared the statue of Perniankhu with his skeleton.

I was amazed to find that the deformities evident in his statue were realistic depictions of his actual appearance. Some other of my favorite discoveries from Giza are a magnificent statue of the priest Kai with his family, like Perniankhu from the Western Field, and four statues of Inty-Shedu, which represent him at different stages of life, from the tombs of the Pyramid Builders.

The mummy of Hatshepsut, now on display in the Royal Mummy Room at the Egyptian Museum, tells a particularly fascinating tale. This mummy was found by Howard Carter in 1903 in the Valley of the Kings, in tomb KV 60. Several decades earlier, and several miles away from KV 60, in the royal mummy cache at Deir el-Bahari, a wooden box containing canopic material and inscribed with Hatshepsut's cartouches was found. Several years ago, as part of a new project to investigate some of the royal mummies using modern forensic techniques, my team and I CT-scanned the mummy from KV 60, and this small box. The mummy from KV 60 was missing a tooth, and to our amazement, there was a tooth inside the box that matched the space exactly. Thus we were able to positively identify the KV 60 mummy as the great female pharaoh Hatshepsut.

More recently, my forensic team and I were able to solve several of the mysteries that surround the family of King Tutankhamun through extensive DNA and CT testing on several known and unknown mummies, some now in the Egyptian Museum and some still in the Valley of the Kings, where they were discovered. One of the skeletons was from a coffin from a small tomb in the valley; this coffin is now on display in the Amarna room on the ground floor of the museum. Through DNA analysis we were able to conclude that this mummy is the father of King Tutankhamun, and identify it as Akhenaten, son of Amenhotep III and Queen Tiye. We have now moved two of the mummies studied, hidden in ancient times in the tomb of

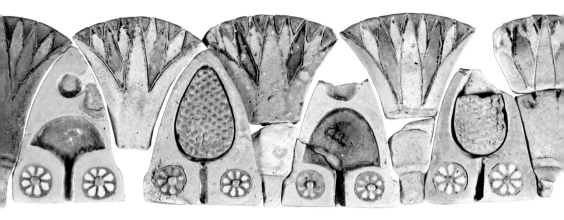

Amenhotep II, to be displayed in front of the Royal Mummy room. One is the 'Younger Lady,' identified through our recent study as the mother of Tutankhamun and the full sister of Akhenaten; and the other is the 'Elder Lady,' now conclusively identified as Queen Tiye.

I am very proud to have all of these discoveries on display at the Egyptian Museum in Cairo. It would make any archaeologist feel proud to have such objects on display for the world to see, in the company of so many extraordinary masterpieces. These pieces tell so many wonderful stories. One of my favorites is a small ivory statuette of Khufu, builder of the Great Pyramid. This statuette was unearthed by Sir William Flinders Petrie, a famous English archaeologist, during his excavations at Abydos in Upper Egypt. The workmen brought Petrie the lower part of the statuette, without its head. Petrie looked at the statuette and realized that the head had been broken off at the neck recently, and must still be nearby. He asked his Reis, the overseer of the workmen, to go to Balyana, the nearest town, to buy sieves. The workmen spent the rest of the day sifting through every single piece of sand until they found the head of the Khufu statuette. Petrie put the two pieces back together and visitors can now see the fully restored statuette on the ground floor, in a small room that houses the treasures of Khufu's mother, Queen Hethepheres. This statuette is the only inscribed representation of Khufu ever found.

This book will help guide you through all the great masterpieces of this museum, from the hauntingly realistic mask of Tutankhamun to the mysterious statues of Akhenaten. Experience all the magic, mystery, and great discoveries in this unique Egyptian Museum, my favorite museum in the world.

Zahi Hawass
Cairo, 2010

The Golden Mask of Tutankhamun

There is nothing in the world greater than this mask; it looks so alive. About 11kg in weight and made of gold and semiprecious stones, a beautiful, bejewelled collar adorns his chest and magical inscriptions run around the shoulders and the back. These are taken from Chapter 151b of the Book of the Dead and are meant to help protect the young king. Tutankamun is seen wearing the *nemes*-headdress, with a uraeus and vulture at his forehead, and his ears are pierced.

The golden mask was discovered by Howard Carter in 1925, covering the head of the royal mummy. At the time, he tried to remove it but was unable to as the resins used during mummification had stuck the mask to the body. Carter finally used tools to remove it and in the process damaged the mummy, breaking it into eighteen pieces.

Tutankhamun died at the age of nineteen and there has been much discussion over the years why he died so young. It has been argued that a hole, visible in the back of the king's head is evidence that Tutankhamun was murdered. However, during our analysis, we found that this opening had been made for the insertion of a liquid related to the mummification process. We also discovered that he had a fracture in his left leg which may have happened as little as one day before he died. Recently, after our DNA and CT-scan studies, we made two important discoveries: first, Tutankhamun's left leg showed deformities, which may explain why 133 sticks used by the king had been placed in the royal tomb. There is even a famous scene of the king leaning on a stick in the presence of his wife. The second major discovery was that Tutankhamun suffered from severe malaria and that this was probably the main cause of his death.

In 2008 – 2009, we made further discoveries relating to the family of Tutankhamun using CT scans and DNA analyses. We have now identified the mummy of Queen Tiye, whose body had remained in the tomb of Amenhotep II since its discovery, and found that the 'Younger Lady,' also found in the Tomb of Amenhotep II, was the mother of Tutankhamun. We also performed a study on a skeleton found in KV55, in the Valley of the Kings, and found that it is, in fact, the remains of King Akhenaten and that he is the father of Tutankhamun. The elder of the two foetuses, found in the tomb of Tutankhamun, was also given a DNA test, which revealed that it was a daughter of the king. The younger foetus was in too poor a condition to be analysed. Due to our work on the elder foetus, we now hope to be able to identify the mummy of the mother and then, perhaps, also the mummy of Nefertiti.

The Statue of Khafre

Every week, I make sure I visit the museum to see my favourite piece – the statue of Khafre. Here, the king can be seen sitting on a lion-legged throne. He wears the *nemes*-headdress, with a uraeus at the forehead, a false beard and a short kilt. His left arm is placed on his left knee, while his right hand is on his right knee, clasped around a folded cloth – a symbol of authority. On each side of the throne can be seen the *sema-tawy* motif – representing the unification of Upper and Lower Egypt. I have walked around this statue hundreds of times and, each time, I find myself isolated and alone with it, thinking about this masterpiece of art, created 4,500 years ago. Although the statue looks to be of one person – King Khafre – it is, in fact, a triad. The king is Osiris in death, while the falcon at the back of his head is Horus; the throne upon which the king sits is the hieroglyphic symbol for Isis.

The Dwarf Perniankhu

This statue of the dwarf Perniankhu, you can see on the ground floor of the museum, close to the statue of Khafre. I will never forget the discovery of this statue in 1987 during our work at the tomb of Nesutnefer, Overseer at the Pyramid City of Khufu, which is in the western field at Giza. The statue shows the dwarf, Perniankhu, sitting on a low chair, without a back. The dwarf is wearing a traditional, curled wig; his face is strong and displays a quiet serenity, strength and power. His eyes are framed in black and the eyebrows are well-defined. The right hand is placed upon his right thigh and holds the *sekhem*-sceptre; his left hand, across his chest, holds a long staff. Perniankhu wears a white kilt with a black belt; his legs revealing deformities. His name and titles can be seen in the two vertical lines at the front of the chair; he is described as, 'One who delights his lord every day, the king's dwarf, Perniankhu, of the Great Palace.'

The Statue of Kai

Another one of my favourite pieces in the museum is the statue of Kai, which can also be seen on the Ground Floor. The statue shows Kai sitting on a high-backed chair. He wears a shoulder length wig, decorated with horizontal rows of curls. Each eye is framed in copper, while his eyebrows are in raised relief. The lips are thin and finely drawn. Below, he wears a *wesekh* (broad) collar, composed of seven horizontal bands of blue and green. Tear-shaped pendants hang from the final band of the collar, whilst a counterpoise can be seen at the back. His right arm is bent across the chest with his hand holding a folded cloth. The left arm is resting on his lap and he sports a short white kilt. Five lines of inscription on the base of the statue provide Kai's titles, including the 'Steward of the Great Estate.'

Kai's daughter can be seen sitting at her father's left leg; she is wearing a wig and a fitted white dress, as well as a *wesekh*-collar of three bands.

Kai's son can be seen standing, embracing the right leg of his father. He holds a finger to his mouth – a sign of childhood – and has short, black hair.

The First Triad of Menkaure

George Reisner discovered five complete triad statues of Menkaure in the King's Valley Temple at Giza. Three of these are now in the Egyptian Museum, while two are in Boston. Here the king can be seen standing, the muscles of his body well defined, wearing the White Crown of Upper Egypt, a false beard, and a short kilt. His left leg strides forward, in the conventional manner. The goddess Hathor, to his right, holds his hand, identifiable by the cow's horns and sun-disc that surmount her wig, and by the inscription below, which reads, 'Hathor, Lady of the Sycamore Tree in all her places.' To his left stands a personification of the Diospolis Parva Nome (district) of Egypt, herself identifiable by the standard above her head.

The Statues of Intyshedu

My other favourite group of statues was found amongst the tombs of the pyramid builders at Giza – the four statues of Intyshedu. These statues all represent the same person at different stages in life. When we excavated the tomb in the upper cemetery, we discovered four statues: in the middle was the main, large, seated statue, to its right was another seated statue, while to its left was another seated statue and a standing statue. All bore the name Intyshedu. As the Egyptians believed in arranging art according to symmetry, it seemed odd that a large, central statue would have two statues to one side and only one to the other. Then, we found the remains of a wooden statue on the right, which had entirely disintegrated. Thus, there were originally five statues: the central statue, most likely along with a standing and seated figure to either side.

The main statue depicts Intyshedu on a backless chair, wearing a black wig. The body is of a strong man; his left hand rests on his knee, while he holds a folded cloth in his right hand. Below, he wears a short white kilt, tied with a belt. On the right side of the chair he is identified as, 'the Overseer of the Boat of the Goddess Neith, the King's Acquaintance, Intyshedu.'

The statue to the left is smaller in size and again shows Intyshedu seated on a backless chair. He wears a flared wig, common in the Old Kingdom. He wears a *wesekh* collar around his neck, painted with three rows of beads, coloured blue and white. His hands are placed on his knees, while his right hand holds a folded cloth. He is wearing a white kilt, tied with an elaborate knot at the waist. This statue depicts Intyshedu in his youth.

The third statue to the left of the main statue shows Intyshedu standing with his left leg striding forward. He wears a short tied white kilt, and holds a folded cloth in each hand. He has a short wig on his head and both eyes and eyebrows slope downwards. He wears a broad collar but, this time, of white and blue beads.

The statue to the right of the central figure also shows Intyshedu seated on a backless chair, his two hands on his lap. He wears a black wig, which reaches down to the shoulders. He wears a broad collar of white and blue. He holds a folded cloth in his right hand and he is wearing a short white kilt.

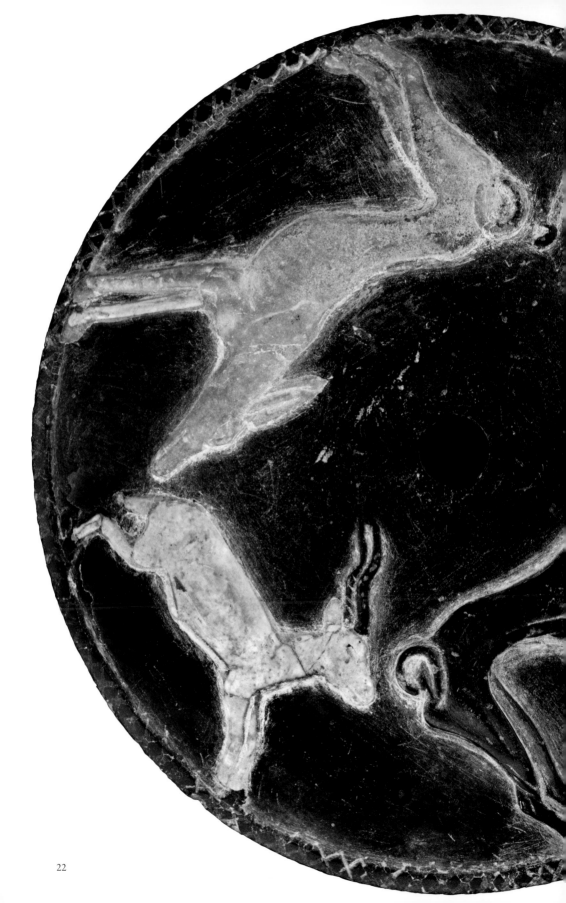

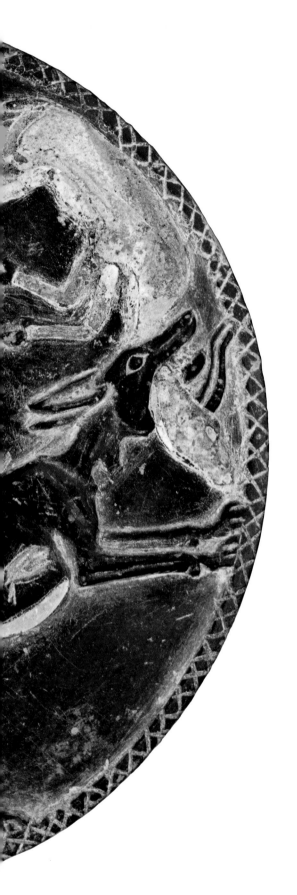

A Hemaka Disc

Hemaka, who lived during the 1st Dynasty, was a treasurer and vizier. His tomb contained many funerary objects, with decorated pieces made of stone, copper, ivory, and wood. These particular objects – known as the Hemaka discs – were found in 1936 by the Egyptologist Walter Emery inside a wooden box; we do not know their purpose, but Emery suggested that they may have been used for weaving, although they may have been used as part of a game. One of the examples bears a hunting scene, showing two dogs and two gazelles, another shows two birds, while the final example displays geometric patterns.

The Porter of the Basket of Niankhpepi

This is a beautiful servant statue. He has wide eyes, that make him seem alive, a short kilt, and his left leg is striding forward. A bag is tied to his back by a strap around his neck, and he holds a beautiful box in his right hand.

The Narmer Palette

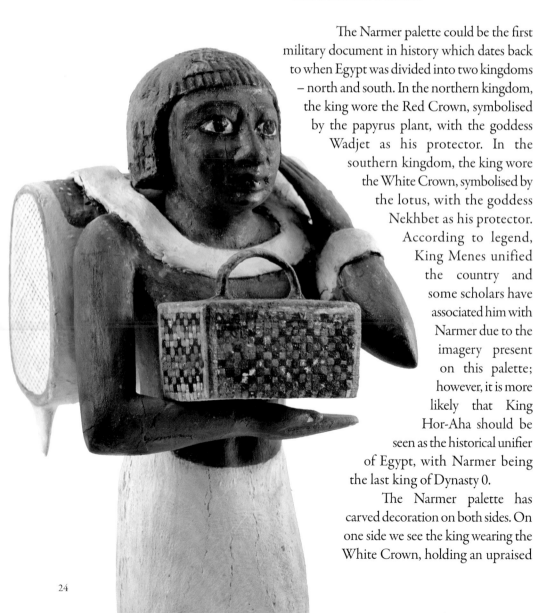

The Narmer palette could be the first military document in history which dates back to when Egypt was divided into two kingdoms – north and south. In the northern kingdom, the king wore the Red Crown, symbolised by the papyrus plant, with the goddess Wadjet as his protector. In the southern kingdom, the king wore the White Crown, symbolised by the lotus, with the goddess Nekhbet as his protector. According to legend, King Menes unified the country and some scholars have associated him with Narmer due to the imagery present on this palette; however, it is more likely that King Hor-Aha should be seen as the historical unifier of Egypt, with Narmer being the last king of Dynasty 0.

The Narmer palette has carved decoration on both sides. On one side we see the king wearing the White Crown, holding an upraised mace in his right hand, while in his other hand he holds an enemy by the hair, ready to smite him. A clump of papyrus is also in front of him, with a prisoner's head tied by the nose. Behind the king is the royal sandal-bearer; his name is written with the symbol of a flower and he holds a vessel for purification in his right hand. In the lower register we see two fallen foreigners, while at the top of the palette are two images of Hathor – human-faced cows with curling horns. The king's name – Narmer – is written in the *serekh* (symbol of the palace) in the top-middle of the piece.

On the reverse side a representation of the king's victory can be seen in the second register, below the two images of Hathor and the name of Narmer. The king, this time wearing the Red Crown of Lower Egypt, walks in procession, his sandal-bearer again behind him. People carrying poles topped with standards, representing Narmer's victory, walk before them. At the far right of this register can be seen two rows of defeated enemies, their decapitated heads placed between their legs. In the register below are two long-necked mythological animals, which represent the north and the south. Two men are controlling the creatures, symbolising the control of the Two Lands, while the intertwined heads represent unification. In the bottom register the king is presented as a strong bull, destroying a fortress and defeating an enemy.

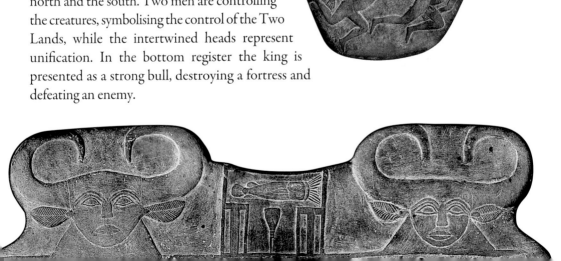

The Khufu Statuette

The Egyptologist Flinders Petrie was excavating in Abydos in 1903 when one of his workmen found the body of this statue, but without the head. After examining the piece Petrie realised that the break was recent, and so ordered his workmen to sift through all the sand in the area until the head was found.

This is the only surviving representation so far known of King Khufu, builder of the Great Pyramid. Despite the fact that the statue is very small, the artist succeeded in expressing the power of the king. Khufu is identifiable here due to his Horus name being preserved on the piece. He sits on a throne, wearing the Red Crown of Lower Egypt, and a short kilt. In his right hand, over his chest, he holds a flail, while his left hand rests upon his left knee. This statue is typically cited as Old Kingdom in date, but after careful study, I believe it to be a 26th Dynasty copy of an Old Kingdom original.

The Sheikh el-Balad

This statue represents the Lector Priest Ka-Aper. At the time of its discovery by Auguste Mariette, an unpopular mayor in the village had died, and when the local workmen looked into the eyes of this statue they believed that he had returned. Thus, Mariette dubbed it the Sheikh el-Balad, The Headman of the Village. The carving shows the artist's great skill: the life-like expression on the face, with his thick cheeks, is emphasised by the copper framed eyes, with quartz acting as the white of the eyes, and black paste for the pupils. These elements combined make it is easy to believe that this man is alive and standing there. It is truly a masterpiece.

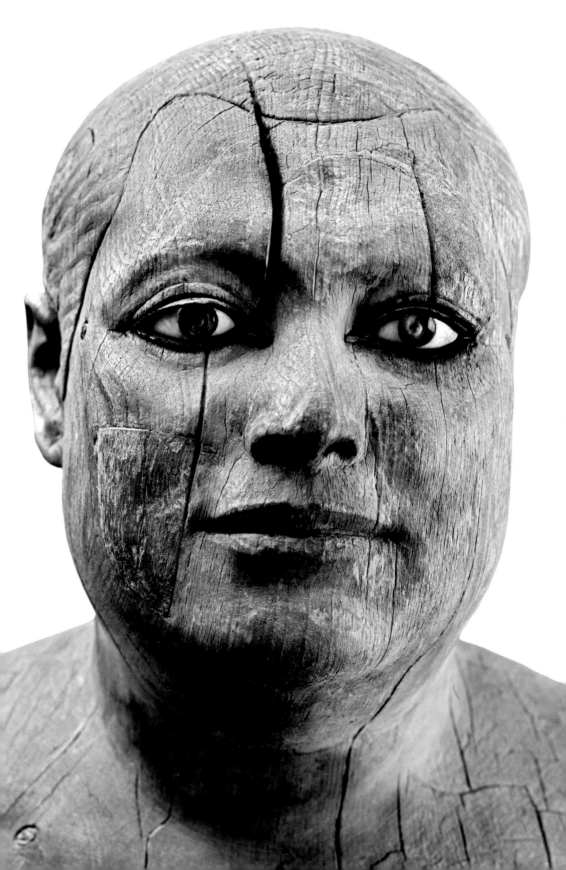

The Meidum Geese

Six geese can be seen here, standing in two groups – one group to the right and one to the left – each consisting of three geese. The four central geese have their heads raised,

while the final goose on each side is eating food from the ground. The geese are painted in exquisite detail, and the artist has shown great skill in creating a symmetrical composition. The artist was also keen to fill the spaces by drawing green grass, and some small flowers.

The *Ka*-Statue of King Hor Auibre

This *ka*-statue of King Hor Auibre was found during the 1894 excavation at Dahshur. It was originally covered with painted stucco, which disintegrated once it was exposed to air. The ancient Egyptians believed that their beings were composed of numerous parts; one such element was the *Ka* (the double or vital force). The *ka* was formed at the same time as the body on the God Khnum's potter's wheel. In order to survive after the body's physical death, the *ka* required the deceased's preserved corpse or a statue to inhabit, as well as a regular supply of food and drink. Thus, the ancient Egyptians did their best to preserve their human remains in order for the *ka* to live for eternity.

Ka-statues were placed inside the tomb where they would receive goods placed on an offering table at the base of a false door, through which the *ka* could magically pass to receive energy from the food. This statue of King Hor Auibre has the hieroglyphic symbol for the *Ka* – two raised arms – above his head, emphasising its purpose. The king is completely naked, although traces of his belt and kilt can still be seen. He wears a tripartite wig that emphasises his ears, and a long false beard. His eyes are made of bronze, rock crystal and white quartz, producing a very realistic effect. His right hand probably held a sceptre, and his left hand a staff. His left leg can be seen striding forward.

The Chapel of Hathor

This small Hathor chapel was made by Tuthmosis III at Deir el-Bahri between the Temple of Hatshepsut and the Middle Kingdom Temple of Montuhotep II. The chapel is rectangular, with a vaulted ceiling decorated with stars. On the back wall is a scene of Tuthmosis III offering to the god Amun-Ra, who sits on a throne. At the front, on the left wall, Tuthmosis is accompanied by his wife, Meritre, before the divine cow and Hathor, while on the right wall Tuthmosis is shown with two princesses. Scenes on either side of the shrine, in the middle, show Tuthmosis III being suckled by the divine cow, followed by scenes of Tuthmosis and the goddess Hathor in human form.

The statue of Hathor as the divine cow, in the middle of the shrine, is inscribed for Amenhotep II, Tuthmosis III's son and successor. Hathor's head is surmounted by a uraeus, a solar-disc, and two short plumes. Amenhotep can be seen twice in the statue: once at the front beneath the cow's head, and a second time presented as a young boy nursing beneath the cow's right side.

The Coffin of Akhenaten

This coffin was discovered in tomb KV 55, in the Valley of the Kings, in 1907 by Theodore Davis. Within, Davis found a skeleton that scholars initially attributed to Queen Tiye, wife of Amenhotep III. However, after further careful examination, they found that it was the body of a king, rather than that of a queen. It was then argued that because the body appeared to be that of a twenty-five year old male, it could be King Smenkhkare; however, the British Egyptologist Alan Gardiner, who studied the coffin, found many epithets that connected it with Akhenaten.

The lower part of the coffin went missing between 1915 and 1931 during restoration works. It was found again in 1972 and put on display in Munich in an exhibition called the Secrets of the Golden Coffin. In 2002 the museum returned the coffin to Cairo.

A Canopic Jar, possibly for Kiya, Secondary Wife of Akhenaten

Many objects belonging to Queen Tiye, Kiya, Akhenaten and Amenhotep III were found in the mysterious Tomb KV 55 in the Valley of the Kings. It has been argued that this tomb was used as a burial place for remains and objects brought to Thebes from Tell el-Amarna after Akhenaten's death. This canopic jar is one of four found in the tomb; it is possible that it was originally made for Meritaten, Akhenaten's daughter, who may have married the enigmatic King Smenkhkare, though many now assign it to Kiya, or even Smenkhkare himself.

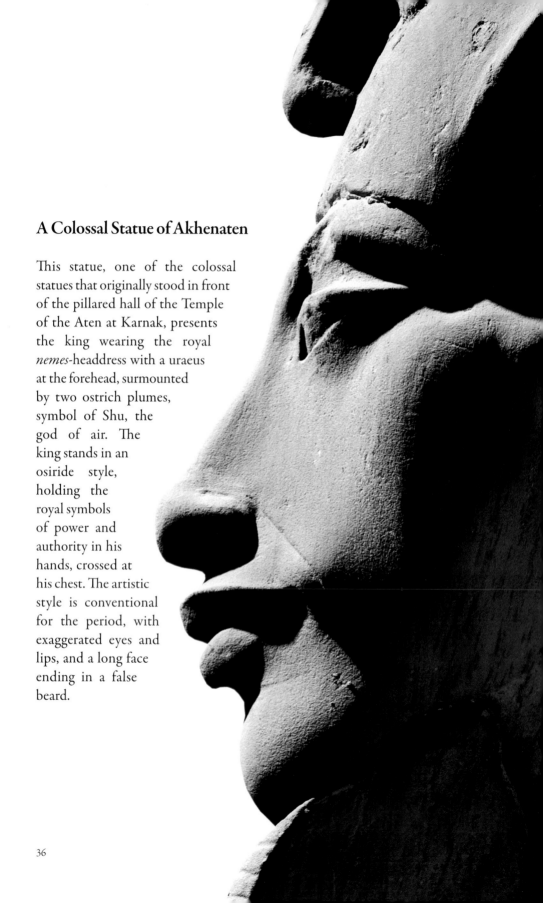

A Colossal Statue of Akhenaten

This statue, one of the colossal statues that originally stood in front of the pillared hall of the Temple of the Aten at Karnak, presents the king wearing the royal *nemes*-headdress with a uraeus at the forehead, surmounted by two ostrich plumes, symbol of Shu, the god of air. The king stands in an osiride style, holding the royal symbols of power and authority in his hands, crossed at his chest. The artistic style is conventional for the period, with exaggerated eyes and lips, and a long face ending in a false beard.

The Royal Mummies

There are two mummy rooms in the Egyptian Museum. One room contains the royal mummies of the late Second Intermediate Period and Early New Kingdom, such as Amenhotep II, Tuthmosis IV, Seti I, Ramesses II, Merenptah, Seti II and the mummy of Hatshepsut. The second room, on the museum's west side, contains mummies of the later New Kingdom and the Third Intermediate Period, such as Ramesses III, Ramesses IV, Ramesses V, Ramesses VI and Ramesses IX. Mummification was practised in Egypt from the beginning of Egyptian history and is even evidenced in the Predynastic Period. The mummy of Nefer, of Old Kingdom date, is an impressive example of early mummification attempts. Over time mummification techniques became more sophisticated. In the New Kingdom it was normal for the body to be dried in natron for forty days and for the internal organs, as well as the brain, to be removed. The body would be packed and wrapped with linen, and covered in resins to help preserve its shape and to stop decomposition. The heart would be left inside the body, however, as it was considered necessary to enter the afterlife.

When the mummies of the kings are moved to the National Museum of Egyptian Civilisation in Fustat, the CT-scan and DNA results for each mummy will be on display, so that visitors can discover how and when they died. At the time of writing, we have so far identified the members of the family of King Tutankhamun, and almost completely identified and examined the mummies of the 18th Dynasty. In 2009 we began a study of the Ramesside royal family, in which we intend to focus on the correct identification of each mummy. We will also be able to discover the exact relationship between the so-called mummy of Ramesses I, currently in Luxor Museum, and the mummy of his son Seti I, or his grandson Ramesses II. The mummies that you see in the Egyptian Museum were discovered in three major cachettes. The first one was found south of Deir el-Bahri, Luxor, in 1881, in tomb 320. In 1871, a member of the Abdul Rassul family was leading his goats at Deir el-Bahri. While chasing one of the goats, he found a shaft inside the cliff. He was able to descend into this shaft and found himself standing in front of a treasure of gold and coffins. The family kept their discovery secret for many years. The Egyptian government moved all forty mummies to Cairo in 1881. When the mummies arrived at the port at Bulaq the customs official looked in his categories of goods for the word 'mummy,' but could not find it, and so did not know how to document the cargo to allow them to enter Cairo. After some thought, he found the entry for 'salted fish,' and so let them enter under this heading!

The second cachette was found in 1898, behind a decorated wall in the tomb of Amenhotep II. It contained twelve mummies, of which nine were moved by Howard Carter to the Egyptian Museum. After cutting a hole in the wall, the mummies of Tuthmosis IV, Amenhotep III, Merenptah, Seti II, Siptah, Ramesses IV, Ramesses V, Ramesses VI, and three unidentified women and a boy were discovered. During our project to identify the family of King Tutankhamun through DNA analysis, we found that the elder unidentified lady from the tomb is Queen Tiye, the famous wife of Amenhotep III, while the younger lady, who was once identified by an English Egyptologist as Nefertiti, is the mother of Tutankhamun.

However, we still do not know her name, and so cannot state for certain which queen she was. The third and most important cachette at Deir el-Bahri was again found by the Abdul Rassul family, and has been dubbed the cache of the priests. After reaching the bottom of a shaft near the tomb of Queen Neferu at Deir el-Bahri, a narrow tunnel full of wooden coffins

was found which dated to the 21st Dynasty, and belonged to the priests of Amun. More tunnels and rooms were found as the excavation work continued. When the Antiquities Department moved these coffins in 1891, they found that there were one hundred and fifty-three coffins inside, but the mummies within had all been plundered.

The Mummy of Ramesses V

Ramesses V was the son of Ramesses IV and grandson of Ramesses III. After a short reign of only four years, Ramesses V died at the age of twenty. Ramesses VI - another son of Ramesses III - succeeded to the throne. Ramesses V appears to have suffered from a skin disease.

The Mummy of Hatshepsut

This mummy was found by Howard Carter in KV 60, in the Valley of the Kings. While assembling all unidentified mummies with their right arms placed across their chests – a royal posture – for the Egyptian Mummy Project, we decided to study some of them with a CT-scan machine. At the same time we also scanned a canopic box from the Deir el-Bahri cachette that was inscribed for Hatshepsut and contained her liver. To our surprise there was also a tooth inside – a molar with a root; and when we examined the mummies we found that it fit exactly into the mouth of one of the royal women. This was a beautiful moment in my life, for although it had happened by accident, I had discovered the mummy of Hatshepsut. After analysing Hatshepsut's mummy we concluded that she had died at about the age of fifty, that she had been obese, and that she had diabetes and cancer. The box that contained the tooth is also on display near the mummy.

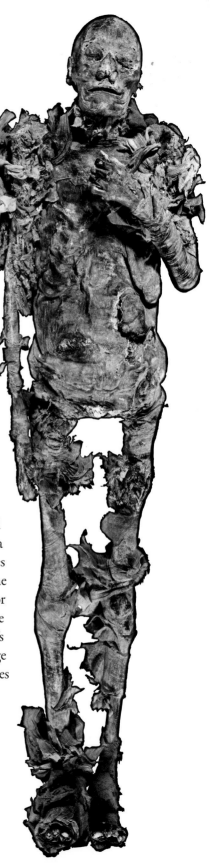

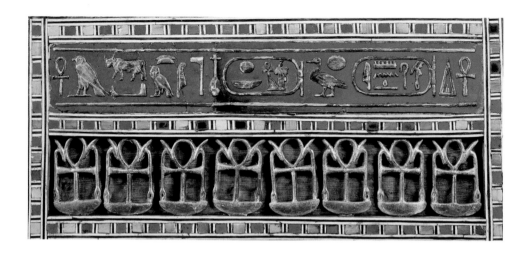

The Funerary Assemblage of Yuya and Tuya

These objects were found by James Quibell and Theodore Davis in Tomb KV 46 – in the Valley of the Kings – in 1905; together they form the virtually intact funerary assemblage of Yuya and Tuya, parents of the 18th Dynasty Queen Tiye, wife of Amenhotep III. Yuya held important military positions, such as Charioteer Commander, while Tuya was Priestess of Hathor and Amun. Although the tomb had been robbed in antiquity, evidenced by the coffins having been opened, the tomb had been resealed following the break-in, preserving the remaining contents for posterity.

The tomb was divided into two sections: the first, to the north, was a store, while the second section, to the south, was for the coffins and funerary objects. The sarcophagus of Yuya was located in the east, and that of Tuya in the west. Yuya's mummy was found within three coffins, all enclosing one another, and all placed within his large sarcophagus. Tuya's coffin was placed within two anthropoid coffins, themselves within her large sarcophagus. Each mummy wore an elaborate golden mask and exquisite collars, and both were provided with four alabaster canopic jars to contain the viscera. Yuya had fourteen shabti statues, compared to Tuya's four, with more than half of these fourteen statues being found inside painted boxes. Each had associated tools made from wood or copper. Yuya's Book of the Dead was also found in the tomb; this was ten metres long, and describes his journey to the next life in detail. Around the sarcophagi were further funerary objects: three lion-legged chairs; a chair that had belonged to Princess Sitamun, daughter of Amenhotep III and Tiye; jewellery boxes; about twenty-seven sealed vessels; fifty-two pottery vessels filled with natron; eighteen boxes of food; and a chariot that had belonged to Yuya.

The Funerary Assemblages of Maiherperi and Sennedjem

The 18th Dynasty tomb of Maiherperi (KV 36) was found intact in 1899 in the Valley of the Kings. Although the tomb is uninscribed, the burial assemblage suggests that Maiherperi lived under Amenhotep III. In life he had been a Fanbearer on the Right of the King, an important honorific position, and a Child of the Royal Nursery, which meant that he grew up with princes, and the sons of important officials at court.

The 19th Dynasty tomb of Sennedjem (TT 1) was found at Deir el-Medina by a villager. Sennedjem was a Servant in the Place of Truth – a person who decorated and excavated the royal tombs in the Valley of the Kings – who lived in the 19th Dynasty during the reigns of Seti I and Ramesses II. After entering the burial chamber, archaeologists discovered that the contents of the tomb were virtually intact. In total, twenty mummies were found within – all were members of Sennedjem's family.

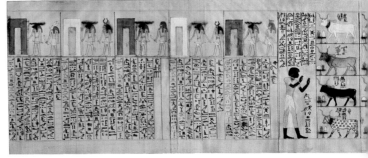

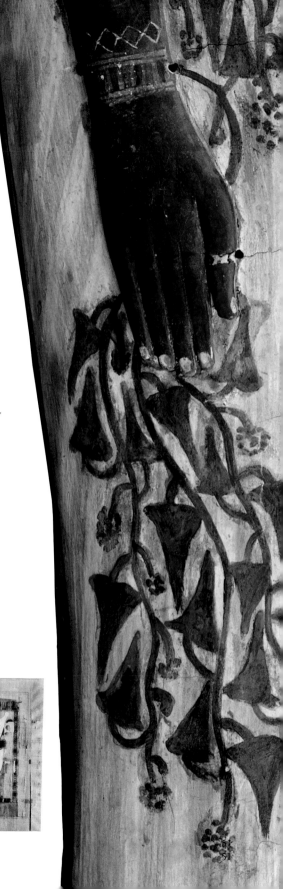

The Sarcophagus of Isis

Isis was the wife of Khabekhent, a son of Sennedjem, from Deir el-Medina. This coffin presents Isis as if she were still alive, rather than in the typical mummiform manner. She wears a heavy wig, with a large *wesekh*-collar below, and is wrapped in a long white tunic, from which her arms emerge. Her hands and arms are decorated with elaborate jewellery, and ivy can be seen along one side of the tunic. Her feet emerge from the tunic at the bottom of the coffin, separated by a short column of hieroglyphs.

The Tutankhamun Collection

One of the most exciting collections in the Egyptian Museum is the funerary assemblage of the golden boy, King Tutankhamun. Tutankhamun became king in the late 18th Dynasty following the death of King Smenkhkare. Tutankhamun was married to Queen Ankhesenpaaten, daughter of King Akhenaten and Queen Nefertiti. Altough raised in the palaces of Amarna during the religious revolution, he made Memphis the new capital city, re-establishing Thebes as the most important religious centre and, further, changing his name from Tutankhaten to Tutankhamun. After his death, Aye, who was a noble of great importance, became king.

Howard Carter discovered Tutankhamun's tomb, virtually intact, on November 4th, 1922. He then spent the next ten years of his life carefully emptying it, and researching the objects within. Altogether he found 5,398 objects. During Carter's time as Inspector of Antiquities he spent five seasons searching for the tomb of Tutankhamun, supported by Lord Carnarvon.

On the morning of November 4th, 1922, a young boy of fourteen was bringing water to the workmen at the valley. When placing his water vessel on the ground he found a step and straightaway ran to Carter's tent and took him by the hand to bring him to see his discovery. Carter began to excavate with his workmen until they found the entrance to the tomb. He immediately sent a telegram to Lord Carnarvon saying that a great discovery had been made in the valley, a completely sealed tomb, and that he would wait for his arrival.

Lord Carnarvon came with his daughter, Lady Evelyn, on November 23rd. On November 24th Carter took Lord Carnarvon to the tomb's entrance to show him the intact seals of the cemetery. Then, as they opened the tomb, Lord Carnarvon asked Carter what he could see inside, and Carter replied with the famous words – 'wonderful things.'

The Corslet of Tutankhamun

This corslet, made from numerous pieces, will have been worn on ceremonial occasions. It completely encircled the torso of the king, and was worn over the shoulders and fastened there. A pendant can be seen below the collar at the front and back. At the front is the god Amun, coloured blue, standing in front of Tutankhamun offering life and the staff of years. Tutankhamun is brought to Amun by Atum, who stands in front of the Goddess Iusaas.

The rear pendant displays the solar scarab, accompanied on either side by two uraei wearing the crowns of Upper Egypt and Lower Egypt respectively; each rests upon two *ankh*-signs. Below the pendants, the lower part of the corslet resembles feathers, made from glass beads.

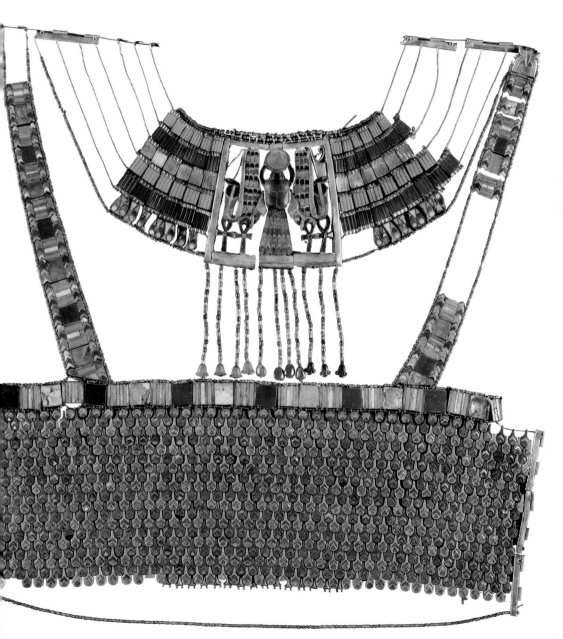

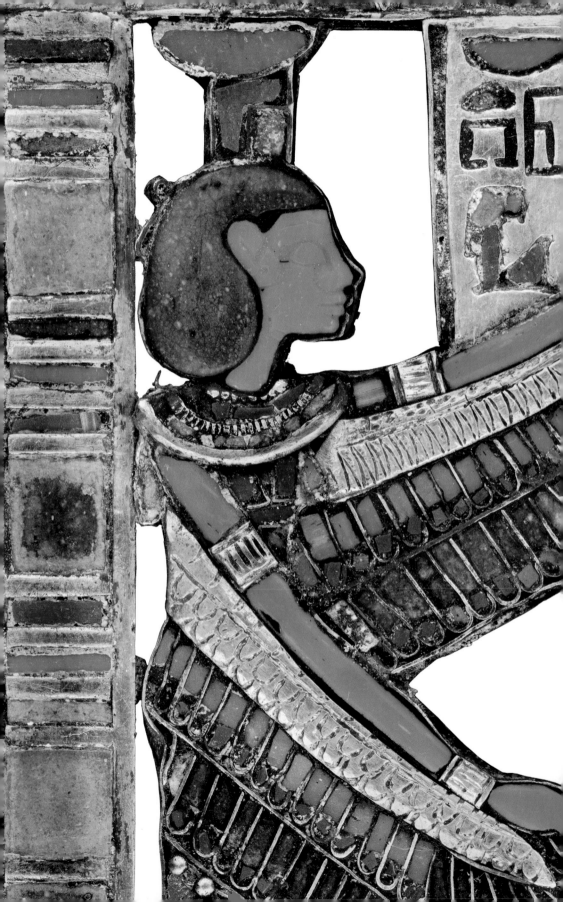

The Head of King Tutankhamun Emerging from a Lotus

Howard Carter found this piece, which represents the king as the god Nefertum, at the entrance of the corridor leading into the tomb. It is probable that this was not its original location, and so it may have been moved by thieves at some point in antiquity. The king's head can be seen emerging from a lotus, which was an important symbol of birth and resurrection in ancient Egypt; he is shown shaven-headed, with pierced ears.

The Mirror of Princess Sathathor Yunet

This mirror is a masterpiece of Middle Kingdom art. The mirror itself is made from silver, while the handle is of obsidian. The handle takes the form of a papyrus flower, and is also decorated with the face of Hathor.

A Pectoral and Necklace of Psusennes I

The pectoral here takes the form of a winged scarab, sitting above a *shen*-symbol, with the cartouche of the king at the front.

The wings are decorated with horizontal rows of precious stones. Chapter 30 of the Book of the Dead is inscribed on the underside of the scarab, in which the deceased asks his heart not to testify against him during the judgement before Osiris. The pectoral is attached to a series of beads ending in a lotus-form counterpoise.

Another Pectoral and Necklace of Psusennes I

This pectoral is framed by alternating precious stones, topped by a cavetto cornice, and with a row of alternating *djed*-pillar and *tit*-knot symbols at the bottom, below a row of sun-discs. A winged scarab can be seen in the middle, and a cartouche of the king above and below, with the uppermost cartouche surmounted by a winged sun-disc.

Rearing uraei also emerge from the sun. On either side of the scarab's wings can be seen Isis and Nephthys, crouching.

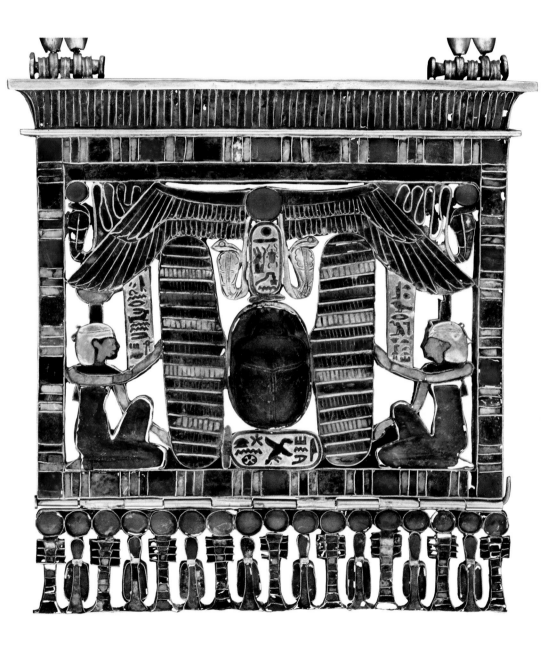